Just Ask the Universe

A No-Nonsense Guide to Manifesting Your Dreams

By

Michael Samuels

The information contained in this book is intended to be education and not for diagnosis, prescription, or treatment of any health disorders whatsoever. This information should not replace consultation with a competent healthcare professional. The content of this book is intended to be used as an addition to a reasonable and responsible healthcare program prescribed by a healthcare practitioner. The author is in no way liable for any misuse of this material.

This book is dedicated to my son, Alexander. You are positive proof the Universe listened and gave me everything I could have asked for in a son.

Contents

Grateful Acknowledgments

To Sharon, Mom, Dad, Eric, Jenn, and Hallie, I could not have asked the Universe for a more perpetually loyal and loving clan than all of you. Thank you for your support.

Special Shout-Out

To my littlest cousin Robbie, you have proven that the Universe shows no age restriction.

Intro

Anyone informed that the Universe is expanding and contracting in pulsations of eighty billion years has a right to ask, "What's in it for me?"

—Peter De Vries (American comic visionary, editor, novelist)

Because it's magic, something out of nothing. The paranormal became normal.

— 311

JUST ASK THE Universe is not a book of New Age gobbledygook filled with empty promises. Angels won't fly from above and touch you while you're reading. Billion-dollar boys' clubs have not passed this book down for generations. This book has not been read by any president. It is not resting in an Ivy League school library. It is not a book that CEOs of Fortune 500 companies have read.

I have no intentions of asking you to practice unusual or tedious rituals. There will be no channeling of your inner chakras or dressing like Friar Tuck.

Just Ask the Universe is a realistic guide to personal development. This journey you are about to embark upon requires you to create a blueprint for self-growth and self-improvement that can help you build a more desirable future.

I'm no sage. I won't preach to you, but I will introduce you to techniques that have clearly worked for me and will most definitely work for you. *You* can have *anything* in this world. Everything you desire is all around you. You just have to learn to ask for it in a precise way.

I have attracted virtuous things in my life (health, money, love and business successes to name a few) because I followed successful people and their ideologies. Success had left me hints along my path in life, but I had to open up my mind in order to find these signs. I have read hundreds of books on self-improvement, spirituality, and the metaphysical. Some revealed "Aha!" moments in my life, and some were a waste of time.

This book would not exist today if it were not for the following "thought teachers" (in no particular order): Wallace Wattles, Anthony Robbins, Rhonda Byrne, Henriette Anne Klausner, Joseph Murphy, Robert Collier, George Anderson, Mike Dooley, William Atkinson, Thomas Troward, Ralph Waldo Emerson, Joel Osteen, John Edward, Ernest Holmes, P. T. Barnum, Benjamin Franklin, Charles F. Haanel, Florence Scovel Shinn, Bruce Lipton, Ralph Waldo Trine, W. Clement Stone, Jose Silva, Emile Coue, and Napoleon Hill.

They all teach a unified lesson: if your thoughts are clear and in harmony with your mind and the truth of your surroundings, your life can be filled with all the richness the Universe has to offer.

I have accumulated the best wisdom from each of these teachers and applied it to my life. The final creation is this book. These methods work, and they have been systematically tested by me and the authors mentioned. The evidence - the things that have entered my life - is indisputable.

I wrote *Just Ask the Universe* because I want to share these invaluable lessons with you. It is truly a secret that was never taught to us in school. I like to think that we are all part of a different school, one that I call *Universe-ity*.

I want you to realize your dreams. Regardless of

your present circumstances, you can achieve whatever you think and believe. I feel blessed to have learned these methods and I would love to share them with you.

If you follow the principles in this book, you will surely get everything you desire.

All you have to do is *just ask the Universe.*

—Michael

Chapter 1
Getting Here

If you do what you've always done, you'll
get what you've always gotten.

— Tony Robbins

I went to a bookstore and asked the saleswoman,
"Where's the self-help section?" She said if she
told me, it would defeat the whole purpose.

— George Carlin

THE UNIVERSE HAS been *at your command* every day of your life. Most people have this idea all mixed up. They believe they are at the mercy of the Universe. Pessimism is just a part of their life, and they believe there is nothing they can do about what happens to them. Nonsense! The total opposite is the truth.

The Universe is completely at your beck and call. It is gracious and compliant to you and will constantly respond to your requests.

It's *your* Universe, and you can grasp it at any time to attain whatever you please. I know that sounds far-fetched, but I have actually witnessed miraculous events in my life that I wouldn't have thought were possible at the time I wrote them down. But these wishes really came true and I certainly believe none of them came about by happenstance. These were not flukes.

As I've learned through experiencing life's labor pains, the Universe will give you anything you want, both the pleasurable and the painful. You can manipulate the Universe however you please, but there are laws and rules you must obey.

Poor Me

I can tell you quite frankly that I wasn't born with this positive mental attitude. I had to learn these beliefs. I originally believed our existence on earth was just a random roll of the dice. I felt people entered and left my life with no lessons to be learned. I felt that if you couldn't see it, it didn't exist. I didn't think there was anything past my square box.

I would listen to interviews of wealthy or famous people and hear them all talk about *their* Universe. I may have been hearing the sounds of their voices, but I wasn't listening to their hidden message. I personally believed anyone who had anything to do with spirituality was batty.

I once watched a biography of a famous comedian, and he said he had signed a check at his father's funeral for twenty million dollars and buried him with it. He said he was going to earn that one day. He ended up making some of the funniest movies ever, and he eventually earned twenty million dollars per picture. I believed it was pure luck.

During an interview with a famous actor/rapper, the journalist asked him how he'd gotten to be so famous at such a young age and how he managed to marry one of the most famous pop singers in the world. He simply answered, "I asked the Universe." I thought this was just another multimillionaire brat who was in the right place at the right time.

I honestly thought these people were out of their minds. After all, they were worth several million (if not hundreds of millions of) dollars, flew in private planes, stayed in luxurious hotels, lived in multimillion-dollar homes, and could eat or go anywhere they desired at any time of the year.

Boy, was I naive. Of course I wanted everything they had—except maybe the fame—and it would be nice to get everything I wanted. What made them different from me?

For the majority of my life I was pretty close-minded. I always wanted people to hear my opinion but when it came time to listening to them, I could have cared less.

This book didn't come to realization by my actions of continuing to be close-minded. As a matter of fact, I made a complete reversal in my way of thinking years back. It took me some time, but I learned that these wealthy people had complete control over their minds.

Looking Back

What now seems like ages ago, I spent a few years stuck in an oppressive and hurtful relationship. I did manage to break myself free of this unhealthy situation. However, I wasn't sleeping and constantly pondered what went wrong. It was easier to blame everyone else around me, point fingers, and say that the relationship was ruined because of others than to take responsibility for my actions. Boy, what a loser!

Looking back and dissecting where I went wrong with my attitude, I learned that what I was doing was merely displacing my feelings. I had to learn that I must essentially see the truth in everything. No matter how bleak things looked back then, I was about to enter a passage in my life that transformed everything about my reality.

The Flower Bloomed

Late one night, I saw an infomercial for Anthony Robbins's Personal Power II program. I knew I wanted to change, but I didn't believe in buying the snake oil. Here was a guy who lived in a castle in California earning hundreds of millions of dollars a year, and there I was, living in my parents' house, lying in my unmade bed, criticizing Tony and belittling his success. I was jaded beyond belief, yet I still mustered up the courage to buy the program. Within thirty days, my entire perception of this world altered. My thought process was transformed. The Personal Power II program awakened my thirst for self-improvement.

There was one turning point in the program in particular that has stuck with me to this day. On or about day 14 of the program, Tony asks you to list your goals—personal development goals, "things" goals, and financial goals. At the time of listening to the program, I followed Tony's orders and wrote down everything I wanted in life.

My goals covered a wide gamut—from the type of person I wanted to be perceived as among my family and peers, to the relationship I wanted to attract into my life. I listed the way I wanted to travel, the homes I wanted to own, and the number of sales I wanted my family-owned business to earn per year. My pen didn't stop for two hours. I got engrossed in writing down as much as I could. I will never forget those two hours of my life. They're among those rare times that you think about consistently that make you smile inwardly. I know a lot of people have had such moments, and this was one of mine.

After I had written down everything I desired my perception changed instantly. I went about my life with a brand-new outlook. My new positive mental attitude was not just about accomplishing an objective but about the value of life I learned on this new road.

It's who you become as a person that matters!

Tony teaches you that getting everything you want on your list by itself can never make you completely happy in the long term because that is not what life is about. Someone could say, "I want a million dollars," and receive it, but that person will never be fulfilled if he or she does not learn one crucial lesson: *it's who you become as a person that matters.*

I know a lot of very wealthy people who seem to have everything, whose circumstances would make any other person elated, yet they are absolutely miserable. None of their "things" make them happy because they are not happy with themselves.

I was finally able to open my mind and listen to

someone smarter than I was. I knew after my thirty days with Tony, I could conquer the barriers necessary to get everything I desired. That lesson alone gave me a permanent feeling of accomplishment.

My Accomplishments

A few years after my thirty days with Tony, the time came for me to move from my parents' house and settle down. I committed myself to a new girlfriend, and we dedicated ourselves to getting married. This relationship was the complete opposite of the one I had attracted into my life just a few years earlier. I had finally found someone who loved me for me.

I found the most perfect home in New York. My future wife and I moved into this perfect home on the same day. We got married within one year of living together.

As I continued to clean out my old room in my parents' house, I came across my "Personal Power" notebook from a few years earlier. With a big smile on my face, I flipped through the pages and found the page with the longest list.

I began to read the list of everything I had wanted to achieve a few years back. After reading the first sentence, I cupped my hands over my mouth to stifle a scream.

Of what I had written down just a few years earlier, 90 percent had come true—from my desires about the way I was perceived among my family and friends to the details of my wife's characteristics and the home I wanted to own. I swear if someone didn't know me they would have said I'd written it down that same day. In just over a couple years, I had achieved practically everything on my list.

What the heck had transpired? What made the Personal Power Goal-Setting Workshop manifest everything into my life?

I mean, there I was, a normal guy from an average home, and I'd written down, "I want to fly on a private plane with my own pilots at my command." Back in the day, when I was thinking this idea, it seemed light years away from life as I knew it.

Due to an unanticipated circumstance, I ended up flying on a Citation X (the world's fastest private plane) just *three* years after writing it down. And the most amazing part was I had no memory of even writing this desire down.

Further down my list, I wrote in detail about the type of woman I wanted in my life. This is what I wrote:

- I want to attract a woman who is marriageable, gracious, loyal, and faithful.

- I want to attract a woman who matches me perfectly mentally, spiritually, and physically.

- I want to attract a woman who does not want to make me over and whom I do not want to make over. There is mutual love, freedom, and respect between us.

- I want to marry a woman with a laid-back attitude. She is five feet nine inches tall and is the same religion as me. She will love me for who I am, in spite of my flaws.

- I want to propose to this attractive woman in front of the Bellagio Fountains in Las Vegas.

- I want to get married to this woman in Las Vegas.

- I want to have a healthy and happy child, who is born during the summer.

At the time I was writing all this, I was seriously hurting from that dismal relationship I'd just gotten out of. While I was writing, I believed there was no way it could possibly come true. I thought to myself, *Who would want to get himself into another relationship after what I just went through?* Right?

I kid you not when I say three years after I wrote everything down, I attracted a woman into my life who possesses every characteristic I listed. We are on the same page mentally, emotionally, physically, and spiritually. She loves me, and I love her unconditionally. I have a child with her who was born in the middle of the summer. And yes, I did propose to her in front of the

Bellagio Fountains; we got married in Vegas; and she is five feet nine inches and of the same religion.

I couldn't make this stuff up. This was pure magic.

And the most fascinating part was that between my breakup and meeting my future wife, I was basically going about my daily life. As these events were occurring, I did not remember that I had written them down previously. There was a massive effort on my part never to think or believe the way I had before. I made a promise to myself that the old patterns of my behavior had departed. My new actions propelled me to get everything I wanted.

Finding More Answers

After reading my list, I knew there was something bigger there. I then realized I hadn't asked for enough. I mean, how did this all work? I could not believe this was some cosmic gamble and I had randomly attracted all that into my life.

> "Action is the real measure of intelligence."
> —Napoleon Hill

I wanted to dig deeper. I would not take this lightly and could not, for one second, believe it was a coincidence. I felt like I had learned the meaning of life in that one minute I spent reading my Personal Power journal. I got hungry for self-empowerment programs and literally read anything I could get my hands on when it came to self-improvement and obtaining everything you desire.

I came across Rhonda Byrne's *The Secret*. I read the book and watched the movie within a day. *The law of attraction*, as Rhonda explains, states that if you think positive thoughts, those thoughts will be attracted to you, and in the act of gratitude, you will gratefully get everything you desire. Pretty genius! There is nothing to dispute; every single word is true.

Although *The Secret* was a powerful book that opened up new doors for me, I wanted to continue searching. I knew that successful people aren't born that way. They all possess a mind-set that gets them everything they want.

I went further back to find the basis of Rhonda's theory and found the two books that I would come to carry with me *everywhere*: Wallace Wattles' *The Science of Getting Rich* (written over one hundred years ago) and Joseph Murphy's *The Power of Your Subconscious Mind* (written over sixty years ago). These two books rocked my soul to its core. And they both talk about the Universe!

I found what I was looking for. The answers I needed were out there, and I began incorporating a little bit of every book and program into my own life. The results continue to astound me daily as the things I desire constantly enter my life.

Now it's your time to shine. What worked for me will most definitely work for you. Without anymore delay, I would like to formally introduce you to the Universe.

Summary

The Universe is at your command every single second of the day.

People who understand the laws of the Universe reap its rewards.

There is a wealth of information just waiting to be discovered by you. These clues are left by successful people.

Your current situation has no bearing on what you can accomplish in the future.

Life is not about getting "things". It's about realizing your dreams and who you develop as a person during this process that matters most.

Chapter 2

Meet the Universe

*There are no limitations to the mind
except those we acknowledge.*

— Napoleon Hill

*Can we actually "know" the universe? My God, it's
hard enough finding your way around in Chinatown.*

— Woody Allen

What Exactly Is the Universe?

SO YOU'RE PROBABLY thinking to yourself now, *What exactly is the Universe?* There are hundreds of shows on TV about the Universe, but when you think about it, they don't give you a full definition of what the Universe is. Is the Universe the blackness you see when you look up into the night sky? Is it the distant stars? Is it the sun? Is it the galaxy? The Universe is all that and more.

The Universe is everything. The Universe is everywhere.

Try wrapping your mind around that.

Everything you observe, hear, breathe, contact, sense, experience, and think is the Universe in motion. Even the stuff you cannot observe, hear, breathe, contact, sense, experience, and think is still the Universe.

It flows through you and around you. You can't escape it because you are a part of it. Every thread of your being is part of the Universe.

The Universe envelops the largest mountain on the biggest planet in our solar system to the smallest subatomic particle in your body. The Universe knows how many cells are working right now in your liver, and it knows the temperature at the center of the earth at this very second. The Universe knows how much water is in the ocean and how many

> *The Universe is everywhere and everything.*

hairs you have on your head. It sees and hears beyond the eyes and ears. The Universe is perpetual.

The Universe is everywhere, and it's responsive to you and everything that it encompasses.

Since the Universe is in all and through all, it can hear all too. We don't have to shout when asking the Universe for something. We are not going to beg or sweet-talk the Universe into doing our bidding. It already is.

How Does the Universe Work?

You may be asking yourself, *How does the Universe give you everything you desire?* The answer is not what you think, and it's quite simple.

It doesn't matter.

After you follow the methods in this book, how the Universe takes it from there is none of your business. You shouldn't overanalyze how it works. You just have to have unconditional faith that it does.

Take a light bulb for example. How does it work? Explain it to yourself. I know you probably can't. I'm not trying to be condescending. Guess what. Neither can I. All I know is that when I enter a dark room and flip the switch, the lights turn on. An electrician might be able to tell you how the lights work. He or she could explain that the electricity flow from the light sockets is cut in two and the switch reinstates the circuit when the two wires are reconnected by a piece of metal. The electrons in the light bulb flow into the sockets, light the bulb, and flow back to their source somewhere on the other side of the meter.

Could you imagine thinking like this *every* single time you turned on a light? You would drive yourself crazy. And deep down, do you *really* care how it works? You hit the switch, and then poof! Let there be light. There is nothing to scrutinize.

It's the same premise with the Universe. I can't tell you exactly how the Universe moves everything toward you; all I know is that it just can and will. There are an infinite number of combinations the Universe will use to bring everything toward you. Listing these combinations would create a never-ending story.

If you follow the instructions in this book and get just one thing your heart desires, that is unquestionable verification the Universe listens and will give you everything you want.

Now that you have been formally introduced to the Universe, let's cut straight to the chase and learn about the connection between the two of you.

Summary

The Universe is everywhere and everything.

Everything you see, hear, breathe, touch, smell, feel, and think is the Universe in motion. Even the stuff you can't see, hear, breathe, touch, smell, feel, and think is still the Universe.

Don't waste a second pondering how the Universe works. It's none of our business.

You don't have to plead or coax the Universe to do your bidding. It is already working for you right this second.

Chapter 3

The Connection

You can build radiant health, success and happiness by the thoughts you think in the hidden studio of your mind.

— Joseph Murphy

Man is a universe within himself.

— Bob Marley

A T THE END of the day, all you have is your mind. Your mind is the only thing on earth that can take the invisible and make it visible.

Your mind is split into two parts: the conscious mind, or reasoning mind, and the subconscious mind which takes orders from the conscious mind.

The conscious mind is the thinking mind, what you use daily to go about your business. You consciously think of getting out of bed, putting on your pants, brushing your teeth, drinking water, writing an e-mail, and so on.

Your conscious mind is responsible for the creative portion of your day. Anything you think about or create comes from your conscious mind. It rests when you are sleeping but is always up when you are awake.

The subconscious, or subjective, mind does everything that your conscious mind does not do. It regulates digestion, breathing, circulation, etc. Could you imagine trying to think about and regulate digesting food? It's physically impossible. We wouldn't even know where to begin.

Your subconscious mind also takes orders from your conscious mind and carries them out without you knowing. It never sleeps and is always alert to your conscious mind's input.

Think of a large commercial airplane. In this day and age of flying, the pilot isn't actually holding the wheel that controls the entire plane while flying. When the plane is in the air, the pilot isn't manually accelerating and decelerating it with two hundred passengers on board. He or she is simply typing in commands on a control panel to raise and lower the plane's altitude and increase or reduce the speed.

Pilots are merely programming the plane to do what they want, and through the unity of a million working parts, the plane complies. Pretty cool, huh?

Your Mind and the Universe

This is how your mind interacts with the Universe. Your conscious mind thinks of something, and your subconscious mind makes it happen by working with the Universe. Your subconscious mind takes everything you say to it literally, so please take extra care when asking your subconscious mind for something.

Could you imagine the pilot of the airplane touching random buttons on the control panel while the plane is in the air? The plane wouldn't yell back, "Not that button!" The plane would carry out the random commands the pilot programs into it. I'm no rocket scientist, but I will bet you anything there would be some nauseous and terrified passengers on that flight!

The plane flows smoothly through the air because the pilot inputs commands in a very specific way. There are instructions involved.

Your subconscious mind is not going to fight back if you tell it something lousy. It will simply carry out your orders. It is not partial to your thoughts, and it just does what it is told.

It takes the same exact effort to program your subconscious mind with thoughts of happiness and abundance than to program it with thoughts of fear and lack.

Your subconscious mind is the link to the Universe. It's not enough to yell out what you crave and wish for the most. You have to program the buttons on your control panel in the correct order with good thoughts for your mind to gain altitude. You have to be *clear* in what you are asking the Universe, and it must be done in the following manner.

First Things First

You cannot think convoluted thoughts. The Universe finds these extremely hard to understand. *Your thoughts must be clear.* You wouldn't send a text message to a friend like this: "Gfeotr ttogoenthietre dlinenetr's." Your friend would probably think you were pocket dialing.

You would send a text message saying: "Let's go out for dinner tonight." Precise. No misspellings, no confusion. You are making a suggestion to a friend about the evening's plans.

It's the same deal when asking the Universe for something. Think of exactly what you want. It can be a specific thing or a multitude of things. Get a clear-cut goal, and don't be fearful. Setting your goals is the fun part, as you'll soon see. They should be exactly what you want and in any type of order.

How Long Will It Take?

Think of a gigantic oak tree with hundreds of branches shooting out of its trunk. Think of the oak tree with thousands of brightly colored leaves budding from the branches. Think of the thick bark that covers every inch from the roots to the tallest peak.

This oak tree didn't appear out of thin air. The Universe didn't just plant the tree standing the way you see it a century ago. That oak tree came from an acorn that isn't any bigger than the end of your thumb. Think about that for a minute. Something as small as the end of your thumb can grow into a tree that is four stories tall with hundreds of branches and thousands of leaves.

The Seeds

It's the same foundation with the Universe. Everything you see in this world started with a thought that has grown to whatever that person intended. Your future is just as you imagined.

Your thoughts are seeds. They must be planted and cared for. You shouldn't over think them. That is basically the same as overwatering a seed. The seed will never grow; it will just get drowned out. You have to let the seed grow by loving and nurturing it. You must water the seeds with the right amount of water and let enough sunshine in. Most importantly, you must have *steadfast belief* that your seed will break through the surface of the soil. That is the greatest care you can give your thoughts – belief.

Clean Up Your Garden

Now, the soil in your garden has to be primed. The rocks have to be removed. These rocks represent negative emotions that weigh you down. They certainly won't let the plants grow. Your mind also has to be cloudless to let the nourishing sunlight through.

Shoo the pests out of your garden. These "mind pests" are negative thoughts that stop your seeds from growing. Don't let pessimism destroy what you planted. When you actually think about it, the words *pests* and *pessimism* sound very much alike. They are technically one in the same, annoying little bits that interrupt your pattern on a great day.

Planting the Seeds

Getting a clear mental image is one thing, but you must place that mental image somewhere in your mind. Just saying you want a brand-new car and then going about your day will not bring you that new car or anything else for that matter. Once this thought has been written down, the Universe has something tangible to work with. Your thoughts and ideas will manifest once your garden is ready to be planted.

We will talk about planting the seeds in your mind soon, but first, we need to get on the same page about two serious pitfalls before we can proceed any further.

Summary

Your mind is split into two parts: the conscious mind, or reasoning mind, and the subconscious mind, which takes orders from the conscious mind.

Your conscious mind directs your subconscious mind to carry out any order you want. To program your subconscious mind, you must use your conscious mind.

Be clear when thinking. Don't let any depressing emotions or negative thoughts weigh you down.

Your thoughts will not spring out of the ground immediately. It will take some time before you see any results. Think of a workout – you won't develop muscles after one workout. It will take a while before you start to see real results.

Chapter 4

Two *Big* No-No's

My actions are my only true belongings. I cannot escape the consequences of my actions. My actions are the ground upon which I stand.

—Thich Nhat Hanh (Buddhist monk, teacher, poet)

Karma's a bitch.

—Anonymous

Universal Laws: A Warning

BEFORE MOVING FORWARD, I would like to add a word of caution to our system. What I'm about to say is paramount in getting everything you want. There are certain universal laws that everything on this planet must obey. You should use the instructions in this book to *benefit you and those you love*. If you purchased this book with the intent to use the principles within to hurt someone or take something away from someone, or if you have these thoughts in your mind, please don't read any further. This book is not for you.

You are strictly prohibited from using the Universe to do your dirty deeds. It won't work. It will stop all development and negate what you have accomplished so far. If you abuse this principle, your garden will be overgrown with weeds, filled with rocks, and infested with pests that will never go away.

Boomerang Precision

The first big no-no is to want something bad to happen to someone else, even if you feel that person deserves it. Do not impose your will on any other person besides yourself. You have no right to do so.

If the Universe feels something is "wrong," it will take care of it. *That is not your responsibility.* Your responsibility is to ask the Universe for great things for you and your loved ones. The Universe will *always* come back around and give you what you want.

If you abuse the Universe's powers to create fear and hurt in other people, the Universe will give you exactly what you are asking for, *but it will happen to you.* If you want to see people fall or fail, or if you wish disease and hurtful things on people, stop at once! You are only doing this to yourself and will stop all advancement in your favor. I cannot stress enough the importance of this universal law. Think of your thoughts as e-mails that have just been sent out into the Universe. When you send these thoughts outward, they get stored in the Universe's database. No one on earth can hack or erase what is on the Universe's servers.

At some point, whether it be a day, a week, a month, a year, or even a lifetime later, that e-mail is going to get sent right back to you—even if you have changed e-mail addresses ten times since that bad thought was sent out. The Universe knows your current address because it is in all and through all. You cannot delete the e-mail once you click "Send." That thought will never be erased from the Universe. The Universe will reply to your e-mail, and it will affect you directly. You can't escape it.

This is why no one on this planet should ever wish anything bad on anyone else. That same thought is going to come right back to you with *boomerang precision.*

Let the Universe take care of everything. You do not have to do anything to anyone, except wish great things and advancement for that person, even if you feel he or she is your enemy or has hurt you in the past. Forgiveness is the best form of revenge. The opposing side's soul is dirty, *but yours is not*. The Universe knows this.

The same goes for bad thoughts directed toward *you*. They have absolutely no meaning. None. Remember, if someone is wishing something bad for you, the Universe knows the score. If you do not accept the bad gift that person sends you, the Universe returns it to the sender. Never forget this.

Quick Exercise:

Think of one person who has hurt you in some way in the past. Now write down something great to happen to him/her. Ask your subconscious mind to give that great thing to this person. You will be amazed at how you feel after doing this. And most importantly, the Universe will be wearing a big smile when you change the way you feel about this person.

What's Yours Is Mine

The second rule is never wish to take something away from someone else. There is an unlimited supply sitting in an infinite stockroom of whatever you require from the Universe.

The Universe will never take something away from someone to give to you *without doing the same to you.*

If you wish to take something or someone away from another person in a competitive and spiteful manner, it will most probably come true. But heed this warning—if you ask the Universe to take something or someone away from another person to give to you, the same universal law will apply to someone else who asks for that same exact thing.

What you get from the Universe today by taking it from someone else through mental force will certainly be taken from you sooner than you think. You will not have ordered the package in the correct way. You have created a chain of events that will simply pass onto another person who desires the same thing. It's a vicious cycle. Don't participate.

This has been specifically demonstrated in my life in the area of business. Coveting the property or accounts of a competitor may land you that property or those accounts, but your gain won't be long term. The same accounts that you so forced the Universe to give you will go to another competitor soon. This has happened to countless salespeople who specifically target and yearn for the accounts of competitors in a spiteful way.

There is enough business for everyone. *Nothing is limited.* As much money as you can ask for and can be made *will* be created a hundred billion times more for you. There is no limit.

If you want a certain house and another person out-bids you for that house, just know that there is a better house for you out there.

If you want another person's spouse, don't ask the Universe to make him or her fall in love with you. Turn the negative feeling into a positive one. You can certainly ask the Universe for attributes and characteristics of that person you desire in your spouse, just don't ask for that person to leave his or her spouse for you. That will only bring bad karma into your life.

Here today, gone today.

Summary

You are strictly forbidden from using the Universe to do your dirty work. It won't succeed. It will stop all growth and counteract what you have accomplished so far.

Do not impress your will on any other person besides yourself. You have no right to do so.

You do not have to do anything to anyone, except wish great increase for that person, even if you feel he or she is your opponent or has offended you in the past.

The Universe will never take something away from someone to give to you without doing the same to you.

You have created a chain of events that will simply pass onto another person who desires the same thing. It's an immoral chain that you should partake in.

Chapter 5

Your Subconscious Wish List

Reduce your plan to writing. The moment you complete this, you will have definitely given concrete form to the intangible desire.

—Napoleon Hill

In a lot of areas of my life, particularly in my teenage years, I began to think about the world, and to think about the universe as being a part of my conscious everyday life.

—Julius "Dr. J" Erving

NOW THAT YOU know what not to do and have a clear thought of what you desire, let's move to the next step and plant the seeds to start the Universe in motion toward you. You must write out your thoughts, just like I did in the Anthony Robbins program.

The "I Want" List

Set aside some quiet time during the day to sit down with a pad and pen—no spouse, no kids, no friends, no cell phone, no TV—just you, paper, and a pen or computer / laptop. First thing, at the top of your list, write, "I Want." On the next line, write in the date. (Remembering to write in the date is very important. I will explain the reasons later.)

Underneath the date, write out the words "I want…" and finish the sentence. Go to the next line. Write, "I want…" again, and then finish the sentence. Keep going until you've written out *everything* you want. Don't hesitate. Just start writing, and write down everything you can think of. As you'll see, this will create a domino effect and build momentum. Your pen will have a hard time keeping up as thoughts fill your mind.

Start every single line with "I want." You are not being covetous or narcissistic. You just are going shopping in the Universe's catalogue with unlimited funds.

If you feel you want to save this as an e-mail draft and e-mail it to yourself, please feel free to do so. Either way works; writing and typing have the same effect. Just get your thoughts down on something.

The Universe is an unlimited storehouse and has everything you could ever dream of stockpiled, waiting to receive your order. Think of a warehouse that spans from the edge of one part of the Universe to the other. It's unlimited, and it never runs out of anything.

The Universe can cover *any* part of your life that you feel is lacking. The size of your request doesn't scare the Universe, so just write it out. Don't hesitate over any desire that comes to mind. Write it out, no matter how silly or far-fetched you may think it is at the moment. Be unrealistic, but not to the point of total stupidity or overblown exaggeration. *Please* don't write: "I want to fly to Mars on a monkey's back strapped to a rocket booster powered by clean fuel to explore the Valles Marineris," or "I want to meet Elvis and have a conversation with him about the inner workings of Google, while eating bacon and cheese omelets."

I can tell you right now, it will not happen. Ever. There is an enormous difference between daydreaming and setting far-reaching goals.

Details

Also, please don't write something as vague as "I want a new car." The Universe will have no clue what you are talking about. Everybody wants a new car. The Universe doesn't have "a new car" stored in its infinite depot just waiting for you. Tell the Universe the exact model, color, and type of car you want. For example, write: "I want a brand-new Red Camaro Limited Edition with black leather interior and a license plate that says 'CHARGED'!"

Trust me, the Universe has that.

Don't write: "I want to fall in love." *Boring!* Instead, write: "I want to meet an attractive person who is my soul mate. I want this person to be caring, passionate, fiscally responsible, loyal, and funny."

Now we're talking! The Universe has these people stored up just waiting to meet you. I know that sounds a bit ridiculous, but I will bet you that your soul mate will pop into your life sooner than you think once this is written down. Only the Universe can make it happen by connecting you two together, and it will occur in the way you least expect.

Don't be monotonous either. Don't tell the Universe: "I want a one-week vacation."

The Universe's is going to raise its brow and say, "Huh?"

Fire it up! Write down, "I want to travel to Australia and go wine tasting while exploring the countryside with my spouse in the middle of summer," or "I want to lie on a beach in the golden sunlight on the island of Maui for a week straight and drink margaritas with my best friend."

Details! It's all about the details, details, details!

For example, if you want to run your own business, use the following model in making your request to the Universe:

- I want to run a successful (pick an industry) business with my (pick a partner).

- I want to have a location at (pick a place, city, state, and/or country).

- I want to make (pick a dollar amount) per year with my business.

- I want my business to afford me a lifestyle that includes (pick what you want your business to provide you).

The following is one of my favorites. Tell the Universe where you want to eat.

- I want to eat at (pick a restaurant) with (pick a partner) to celebrate a romantic evening.

- I want to eat in (pick a city) with five of my best friends.

Tell the Universe which cities, states, or countries you want to visit. Tell the Universe how long you want to visit them.

- I want to visit (your dream place) in (pick a month) and (do what there).

How do you want to travel? By car, boat, airplane, or all three? Tell the Universe who you want to meet and what sights you want to see there.

Complaining

The Universe is at your disposal, but it *abhors* whiners. Do not under any circumstance complain to the Universe about your troubles. Every thought directed to the Universe should focus strictly on the positive and the effect you want.

For example, don't tell the Universe:

- I want a new career because I'm miserable at my current job.

No-no! Say something instead that will bridge you to the solution you are looking for. Do not acknowledge the muddy waters. Remember we need inspiration, not pessimism. Write,

- I want to change careers and have my new boss acknowledge my abilities.

- I want my new career to create total abundance for my family and me.

- I want to make $250,000 in my new career and have a company car with four weeks vacation.

- I want my colleagues to trust me and appreciate the job I'm doing.

This is the correct way to ask the Universe for something. Now, please understand that this is not going to happen tomorrow. Chances are you will be at the same job you are currently employed in for some time, and this is fine. Now that the Universe knows the "I want", it will someday present an opportunity to you. When that opportunity arises, take it and be thankful. Also be mindful that you cannot continue to be miserable at your current job. Be gracious at your current position until the right opportunity comes along. Being congenial today allows the Universe to present you with chance you are looking for.

For Other People

The Universe loves when you want things for other people too. Do not hesitate to want things for people in your life, especially those whom you love dearly.

Tell the Universe what type of relationship you want to have with your friends and family. Tell the Universe what you want for your family. And don't say, "I want my family to be ok."

The Universe will wrinkle its nose and tilt its head. Write instead, something like the following:

- I want my parents to have a strong and fulfilling relationship for many years to come.

- I want my parents to purchase a beautiful second home in a warm climate with a relaxed setting.

- I want my parents to feel safe and comfortable as they age.

- I want my family to live in total abundance in health and wealth.

- I want my brother to live in a one-million-dollar custom-built home close to me.

- I want the relationship between my wife and sister-in-law to always be close and carefree.

- I want my child to get good grades in school and always have a great set of friends who influence him positively.

The Universe is listening to you. There is nothing that is off-limits.

New Page

Now, after you've finished your unbelievably awesome "I Want" list, let's start a new page.

You're probably thinking to yourself, *I just wrote down everything I wanted. Now I just have to wait for the Universe to bring it to me.* Sorry, my friend, if it were that simple, I'd probably end the book here, but it's not *that* quick and easy. Nothing in life ever is.

On the new page, write in the date. Below the date, write "I gratefully received it."

The "I Gratefully Received It" List

Now, write out *everything* you've *received* in your lifetime and end it with "I gratefully received it." You wouldn't be a human being if you didn't receive something. Every person on this planet has gotten at least one thing, whether it's a loaf of bread or a desired job. You have to be specific on this list as well. For example, your list could look like this:

- I wanted a Honda Civic, I gratefully received it.

- I wanted a healthy child who loves me uncondi-tionally, I gratefully received her.

- I wanted a loving and supportive spouse who cares about me, I gratefully received her.

- I wanted to drive across country in an RV with my family, I gratefully received it.

- I wanted a secure job close to my house, I grate-fully received it.

Write down everything that you have accomplished and everything that has entered your life. Think as far back as you can remember, even before grade school.

The following rule is vital though: only write down

positive things that entered your life. Don't write down, "I wanted the girl who stole my boyfriend to get hurt, I gratefully received it." Writing down the negative thoughts only intensifies the negative emotions in your life. Pessimism will not bring anything good closer to you. It actually has the complete reverse effect. Only positive stimulation can truly move good things in your direction.

Once you have completed the "I Gratefully Received It" list, sit back and take a nice deep breath.

Can you believe that the Universe has been working for you your entire existence? Since the day you were born, the Universe has given you everything that you ever wanted. You have been attracting everything into your life without even knowing it.

Use the "I Gratefully Received It" list as a stepping stone to your new list of "I Wants."

Now before continuing on to the next chapter, put the book down and *just start writing*. Don't put it off a day or week. The Universe is listening *now*. It knows you're reading this book. It wants to place your orders. Start attracting a desirable future without delay and the momentum will take over from there. You are going to have a blast doing this, so don't dawdle for a moment. Begin immediately and let your mind kick into high gear. Go for it!

Summary

Thoughts are things. Write out your thoughts in great detail on your "I Want" list.

No matter what your position may be today, whether financially, emotionally or physically, write out what you want that would create your ideal world.

Don't complain to the Universe about your hardships. It will only exacerbate the issues you think you have. Only write down positive aspects on every section of your future life.

You should be grateful for everything you write down in your "I gratefully received it" list.

Put the book down and begin your "I Want" list instantly.

Chapter 6

Conversations with Your Best Friend

The great secret possessed by the great men of all ages was their ability to contact and release the powers of their subconscious mind. You can do the same.

— Joseph Murphy

I believe people can move things with their minds.

— Justin Timberlake

YOU'RE PROBABLY LOOKING at the remaining pages of this book and thinking, *That should be the end of it, right? I made my list. Let the Universe take it from there.* Well, we aren't quite done yet. The fact is we're just getting warmed up.

Making the list was just planting the seeds in the garden. I hope you didn't just plant five seeds, but five *hundred*. Don't sit next to your garden now waiting for the seeds to sprout. And most definitely do not start watering the seeds every five minutes. Remember what I said about over thinking your thoughts? You'll drown them.

You have to cultivate your thoughts and know the Universe is doing its job. The seeds are out there in your garden right now. The Universe knows your list is alive.

Now that you have your list, you've come to the more relaxing part of *Just Ask the Universe*. Go into a dark room, and sit on the floor. Put your legs into a pretzel shape, press your three fingers to your thumbs, close your eyes and calmly say, "Ommmmmm."

I'm just playing with you. Remember how I feel about New Age rituals. *Yuck.*

Actually, you only need part of that exercise. When you are ready for bed, go into your bedroom, or wherever you sleep, and turn off the lights. No, don't start analyzing how the lights get turned off. We covered that in chapter 2.

Hop into bed with a big smile on your face because you are about to *really* connect with the Universe.

Don't watch TV before you fall asleep. You need to be completely relaxed to do this next part. Your mind has to be totally focused. Watching mindless reality TV—or anything for that matter—will interrupt the progress we've been making so far.

Now, close your eyes, like you do every night when you try to go to sleep, and think. Don't think about what happened at work today or what your mother-in-law said at dinner. Think of your "I Want" list.

Go down the list and ask your subconscious mind for everything on your list. Do this with a big, relaxing smile on your face knowing that your subconscious is listening.

Ask your subconscious mind to carry out all the things you want. You can even call your subconscious mind by whatever name you conjure up. Your subconscious is your best friend. He/She is also best friends with the Universe and will be able to carry out everything you want. Name your subconscious something you really like or pick a name that will always bring a smile to your face.

Remember the airplane example I gave earlier? The pilot wasn't randomly hitting buttons to guide the plane. He or she gave the plane commands to carry out.

Your Subconscious is your best friend.

Give your subconscious mind actions to perform. Hand the "I Want" list off to it. Go down your list mentally, and literally tell your subconscious mind everything you want. You are now programming your subconscious mind.

You are caring for and watering the seeds. Asking your subconscious to execute your orders is like sunlight shining on your seeds. Speak to it like it's your best friend. Literally say, "Hey there, (Name), it's me again. I would like to first thank you for giving me everything I ever wanted up until this point. But I'm going to ask you for more. I want..." and then fill in the blanks from your list. Don't be nervous. Your subconscious mind will listen to everything you are saying. It will take everything exactly as you mean it, so really try to represent what you want.

Don't fret if you only manage to ask for a couple of things before falling asleep. Your subconscious mind never sleeps and is always working. Remember, as we talked about earlier, your subconscious is controlling many of your body's vital functions while you sleep.

Befriend your subconscious. Trust me, it's a friend you'll need. It will collude with the Universe on your behalf and start moving everything toward you.

Summary

Give the commands of your "I Want" list to your subconscious mind before you fall asleep.

Only program things you absolutely want in your future. Don't think about things that annoy you or distract you from getting the things you desire.

Don't worry if you fall asleep before you are finished with your list. Your subconscious mind is always functioning.

Chapter 7

Believing Is Seeing

*To think health when surrounded by the appearances
of disease, or to think riches when in the midst of
appearances of poverty, requires power; but he who
acquires this power becomes a MASTER MIND.
He can conquer fate; he can have what he wants.*

— Wallace D. Wattles

*It's the repetition of affirmations that leads to
belief. And once that belief becomes a deep
conviction, things begin to happen.*

— Muhammad Ali

AFTER A FANTASTIC night of sleep, you open your eyes with a big smile on your face. You sit up in that wonderful, comfortable bed. The sunlight is peeking through the shades. Birds are singing a lovely song outside your window.

You look around your room, and lo and behold, everything you asked for is right there in your room waiting for you! It's all there, neatly piled up in the corner—the new car, the money, your dream catch (if he/she is not already sleeping right next to you). All the seeds have grown into your full-blown dreams overnight.

You know I'm not serious, right? Although your dream catch might be snoring deeply right next to you, everything is unchanged from the night before. The same pictures of your family and friends are next to you on your night table, and your alarm is snapping you out of bed with that awful buzzing sound.

You are probably saying to yourself, "That *Just Ask the Universe* book was rubbish. It did zilch for me. I wrote down everything I wanted; I asked my subconscious mind for everything last night right before I fell asleep, and here I am, getting ready to go to work on a rainy Monday morning…and my back still hurts!"

Hold on, partner! Don't greet the morning with your customary sigh. Remember, the Universe detests whiners. In the history of the world, has a seed ever sprouted a tree to its full-grown size overnight? Never,

ever, *ever*. Nothing, absolutely nothing, has ever come to realization overnight.

It could take days, weeks, months, or even years for the Universe to carry out all your orders on your "I Want" list. This is okay. Instead of waking up dreary and puzzled when your dreams will be fulfilled, be thankful. Understand that you had an amazing conversation last night with your true best friend, your subconscious mind.

Since you presented your subconscious mind with your orders, it has been working hand in hand with the Universe to give you everything you want. Both your best friends have begun to carry out everything you asked for. They are eight hours ahead of you. The package was mailed. *Stop* worrying.

Your subconscious mind is now in tune with the Universe, which is already planning on moving everything you desire toward you.

Now that you know the Universe is already moving everything you want in your direction, shouldn't you be happy? You are on the right track to getting everything you want. Picture your "I Want" list as you go about your day, but don't overanalyze it. Focus on the individual "I Wants," but don't get neurotic about them. Begin to live with purpose, believing you are getting everything on your list.

This is an essential point in *Just Ask the Universe*. You have to have unyielding confidence that you are going to get everything you want even if it doesn't seem that way today.

The list and conversation were not wishful thinking, but everything you desire certainly will not just plop into your lap the next day. You have built nice groundwork to get everything you wish for. The soil has been primed for your seeds to grow.

When apprehension overcomes your mind during the day, revert back to your "I Want" list.

Don't think for a second that the list is just some dark-blue ink sitting on a memo pad. The list is real; however, you have to *believe* it is real. Seeing is not believing. It's the total opposite. You have to *believe* in order to *see*.

Believe your list is manifesting. Don't just get into your beat-up Honda Civic. Think about getting into that Dodge Charger you wrote down on your list. It may seem odd now, but begin believing the things on your "I Want" list are all around you, even though you may feel you are decades away from seeing, feeling, smelling, or touching them. They *will* become a reality sooner or later.

> *You have to believe in order to see.*

Build Your Own House

As Henry David Thoreau said, "*If you have built castles in the air, your work need not be lost; that is where they should be. Now put the foundations under them."* Think of the next few years like you are building a house with your hands. You can't build it in a day—this would be physically impossible. You can, however, lay one brick perfectly and cheerfully every single day. By laying a brick perfectly every day of the year, in one year or less, you will have the perfect house that you built all by yourself.

Believing in yourself and your list every day is laying those bricks perfectly. Believing is sowing your seeds. That your list will spring into your reality is a given. It will just take some time.

Focus on that perfect house by laying that brick perfectly every day. Focus on the seeds in your garden, but don't over think them. Focus on your goals and what you want to manifest into your life.

The funny part is you probably will not even be aware of your "I Wants" when they begin happening to you. You'll probably forget you even wrote them down. This is where the date of your list comes in handy.

I Now Have "I Haves"

As many times as you like, whether it is every day, every week, or every month, go through your "I Want" list. You will begin to see the "I Wants" really becoming "I *Haves*."

As the seeds start becoming plants and your thoughts become reality, write down the date next to the things as they enter your life. Write a small note next to each about how you received it, for example: "I want to own and operate a bakery with my sister that will sell delicious cupcakes and cookies. (I gratefully received it on Friday, July 30, when we took the necessary steps to starting our very own Bakery.)"

> *You can't build a house in a day, and a tree won't grow overnight. Everything takes time.*

You will be astounded by the things that have entered your life. It will seem like pure magic when you read them off your list.

Even more important, do not get discouraged whatsoever over things that have not happened yet. You can't build a house in a day, and a tree won't grow overnight. Everything takes time.

No Time Line

There is nothing wrong with setting a specific time to accomplish a goal and have the Universe supply it for you. Setting a time line does work, but on very specific items. It is like overnight shipping—some items are too large to ship overnight and may take time.

> *The great things you asked the Universe for will not enter your life a second earlier or a second later than you are supposed to receive them.*

The Universe will ship your "I Wants"

when you are ready to receive them. The great things you asked the Universe for will not enter your life a second earlier or a second later than you are supposed to receive them. Etch these words into your daily habits. The Universe knows the exact time you are ready to receive everything you want.

Do not get discouraged if the thing you expect to have doesn't arrive on the exact date you wrote down. It probably will not arrive in time, and that is okay.

Last year, a great friend of mine wrote down in June that he wanted three new accounts for his business by October 31. He worked diligently on getting these accounts, and he knew the Universe and his subconscious were both listening to him. Long story short, October 31 came and went, and he didn't even have one new account, let alone three.

A few months passed, and the New Year came. Shortly after the New Year, he received a call from a potential client who was ready to enter into a contract with his company as of February 1. Not two weeks later, another potential client called him and said they would like to give him one division of their account, but they would also like to implement his services in another division of a different property.

Three accounts did arrive, but four months *after* my friend set the specific date for himself. In the four months after my friend set a goal for October 31, he did not get dejected whatsoever. He pressed forward, knowing the Universe would give him what he wanted at the exact moment he was ready to receive it. The Universe never disappoints.

The Universe does however take its time. Don't become disheartened or lose your focus. Keep on keeping on. You will get what you want when the Universe is ready to ship your wishes into your life.

Adding More "Wants"

As you manifest your seeds into everything you want, you can revisit your list as often as you would like and add as much as you want. Remember, always add, never subtract. Adding will only present the Universe with more of what you want.

Consistently go back to your list, whether it is daily, weekly, or monthly. Go down to your last "I Want." Now write in the date you are visiting your list. Continue to add more "I Wants" that are in tune with the times.

If you meet a certain goal, have some more fun and just up the ante. You married the person you wrote down; ask the Universe for great characteristics in your future children. You received that wine-tasting summer vacation in Australia; how about asking the Universe for an island-hopping adventure in the Caribbean with your best friend? You finally opened that family-style Italian restaurant, and the neighborhood loves it; what about another location? Keep going! Always reinvent yourself and your list for the better. If the recipe worked the first time around, it will undoubtedly work again. Bet bigger!

Summary

Your thoughts are not going to manifest themselves to things overnight. Everything is going to take time.

Do not be discouraged when you don't have the thing you want. The Universe will not let you down and will send you the thing you want at the right time.

Believe you are going to receive everything you ask for. Begin to live your life with the utmost faith that your subconscious mind and the Universe are working together to manifest your dreams.

Revisit your list frequently to see if what things have entered into your life. When you come across a dream that became reality, put the date you received it next to it.

Continuously add to your list new "I Wants" that are in tune with the times.

Chapter 8

Think and Thank

The more gratefully we fix our minds on the Supreme when good things come to us, the more good things we will receive, and the more rapidly they will come; and the reason simply is that the mental attitude of gratitude draws the mind into closer touch with the source from which the blessings come.

—Wallace D. Wattles

His personality is so magnetic, he is unable to carry credit cards.

—The Most Interesting Man in the World

RIGHTFULLY SO, THE Universe expects a "thank-you"—lots and lots of thank-you's. As a matter of fact, the more thankful you are about receiving what you want, the faster it will come. And so will the rest of your subconscious wish list.

Thank the Universe as much as you can—morning, noon, and night, breakfast, lunch, and dinner. Don't stop thinking and thanking. Be thankful to everybody you know. Be gracious for living that day. Be thankful for the Universe listening to your requests. Let gratitude seep from every pore of your body. The Universe likes this and will continue to give you more. If you don't have gratitude, your subconscious wish list will be in vain.

There will be times when you want something, and you do everything in this book to get what you want, but it turns out someone else gets that thing before you do. I can tell you now, that thing you so strongly desired was never meant to be yours in the first place. The Universe will instead give you something so much bigger and better.

I'll give a perfect example when it comes to business. A family friend worked incredibly hard to get a specific account that was going to propel her business into the stratosphere in a certain lucrative market. For two full years, she pursued this one property and offered everything she could. She believed she was a shoo-in to win this proposal.

It turns out my family friend's efforts ended

unsuccessfully. Some unknown force at the property had secretly been working against her the entire time she was bidding for the business and sabotaged the deal. She didn't get upset for one second; nor did she doubt herself. Instead, she thanked the Universe for the experience and continued on.

She was thankful and certain that a much larger flower was going to blossom for her business. Whether that time was a day, a week, or a year, something was going to come her way that was bigger than this one account she had wined and dined for two full years. Less than six months after losing this

potential client, she won a different bid from another account. This new account was much smaller than the previous one, but she was so grateful for receiving it, something magical happened.

The new client was part of a parent account that was *much* larger than the one she had previously bid on. Because of her positive mental attitude and pressing-ahead approach, this new account began to utilize her services in a citywide rollout to all their other properties. This was almost a year after she lost the first bid.

Because she was not bitter whatsoever after losing the first bid, she could be grateful to the Universe, knowing her company's sales would skyrocket soon. And they absolutely did. Her sales in that one market blossomed so magnificently she would have never taken the first bid over this new property any day of the week. Gratitude is the key.

Attitude of Gratitude

You must maintain, through thick and thin, the right *attitude of gratitude*, even if you do not get what you want. You cannot feel the Universe cheated you or screwed you over if you do not get what you want at the exact time you want it.

Be grateful for everything—from the steps you take in the morning to your "I Want" list at night.

Your lists are living, breathing gardens with seeds growing in them. The Universe's storehouse never closes. You have to keep growing and adding more to your list as you acquire the things you want. You have to think and be magnetic.

Keep talking to your subconscious mind every night. Continue to hand off commands to it. Be thankful for everything. You will only stand to gain from your attitude of gratitude.

Summary

Be thankful and gracious for everything and everyone, everyday.

The more grateful you are, the more in-tune you become with the Universe.

By maintaining an attitude of gratitude, even when the chips are down, the Universe knows the right time to manifest your dreams. You must continue to have persistent trust that the thing you want is coming to you.

Be magnetic! You will only stand to gain.

Chapter 9

The Land of Enhancement

The reason why the universe is eternal is that it does not live for itself; it gives life to others as it transforms.

— Lao Tzu (founder of Taoism)

Expecting something for nothing is the most popular form of hope.

— Arnold Glasow (humorist)

NOW LET ME be very clear. When I say you are going to get everything you want, I really mean it. But, and this is a big but, you will have to do something *monumental* to receive the thing you want.

The Universe will not give you something for nothing and you are certainly not superior over any other person you deal with. The Universe does not show favoritism. You must give *every* person more in worth than you obtain from them. Nothing in life is free and when the Universe delivers your "I want", you will have to give something valuable in return.

The text in this book may not be worth the money you paid for it. However, if the *ideas* mentioned in *Just Ask the Universe* result in all your wildest dreams come true, then I have absolutely served my purpose. I have given you tremendous worth for the small price you paid. I have enhanced your life. You have to do this with *everyone* in order to get what you want.

For What It's Worth

Let's say for the sake of argument that you really want a rare fabric for a new clothing line you want to start. You want this clothing line to be super-successful and the product offered is exclusive to a select clientele. Write it down on your "I Want" list, ask your subconscious mind before you fall asleep to give you the superlative textile to make your business successful, live with the image of this beautiful fabric in the most optimistic way that it is being created somewhere on this planet and finding its way to you. After developing the notion, have the most complete and automatic conviction that the textile is on its way. Receive it mentally.

In an infinite number of combinations, the Universe will sort out the necessary steps to get you this choice textile to make your business flourish. The transaction will be just as much of a benefit to the person bringing you the cloth as it is to you.

Now, let us say that the precious material you want is only found in a certain region of the world – the Amazon Rain Forest. Far fetched? Possibly. However, your "I wants" will come from the farthest reaches on earth and will be brought to you by the most unlikely person. You will have never heard of this person before and you will have never expected it from them. Do not forget that the Universe is everywhere and everything and it can *connect and affect* all that is necessary to get you what you want.

Now, stick with me on this example. This illustration is all about giving people more in worth. Perhaps you own a fifty-inch flat screen television (a previous "I want" that has now become an "I have") which is priced to be worth several thousand dollars at any major retailer. A tribal leader from the Amazon Rain Forest travels to you with a package of fine textiles you were asking the Universe for. Through the art of persuasion you ask the lead tribesman to give you the package of pricey cloth for the fifty-inch flat screen television. You played the tribesman for a fool. He has no use whatsoever for this flat screen television when he takes it back to the Amazon. Unless he already has a satellite hooked up on his thatch, it has zero worth for him and will add nil to his life. You didn't handle the transaction correctly.

Now, instead of giving him the flat screen TV you decide to instead give him a crossbow with a large holster filled with several arrows worth a few hundred dollars for the same high-quality fabric. He has made a good buy. There is use for a crossbow in the Amazon and when used properly, it will be able to supply him more rations and goods to trade. This weapon will add to his life in every way. The exclusive material has made its way into your hands and now you can begin production for your clothing line. The transaction was used for his benefit and yours.

> *Give every person more in worth than you take from them.*

Give every person more in worth than you take from them. You will be asking the Universe for that deal in the correct manner.

When interacting with people who are introduced to you by the Universe, they must feel the idea of *enhancement* from you.

Enhancement is what everyone is always looking for and their behaviors are established by the need for *more*.

More abundance, more attraction, more ideas, more comfort, more awareness, and more satisfaction.

There is nothing wrong with the universal law of more. Everyone desires growth and people will be attracted to you if you can give them more of what they want. Give everyone the idea that you will enhance their lives and you will never lack anything from your "I Want" list. By giving more to all, you will consistently get your "I Wants".

Regardless of how small a deal may be, even if it's only giving a piece of gum to a friend, put into it the intention of enhancement. Make sure that the people you interact with are imprinted with this notion.

The Autograph

My youngest cousin was fanatical about a popular young musician. My cousin's primary goal was to meet this one artist who has brought so much pleasure to his life. Not only did he want to meet him, but he wanted the artist to say something directly to him, and not just "*hey*". The artist was appearing on a live television show in New York City and it was my cousin's task to get this artist to notice him. My uncle and aunt said he was absolutely nuts and there was no way the artist was going to notice my cousin in a sea of boisterous teenagers.

About a month prior to the appearance, my cousin wrote his desire down on his "I Want" list, asked his subconscious mind to make this happen and believed he was going to get the attention of this artist. Time came and he trekked into the city to meet his idol.

The artist hopped off the bus and the crowd went bananas. My cousin knew the artist's favorite color and wore that color sneaker to the event. My cousin took off his sneaker and waved it at the performer with a smile and calming look on his face.

Out of the thousands of kids in attendance, the performer locked eyes with my cousin and made a bee line to him. He grabbed his shoe and piped "*Cool shoe, man!*", then he autographed the sneaker. My cousin thanked him tremendously, gave the artist a shoe box with the same exact color sneaker and said "*I knew your favorite color, and I knew you would love these.*" The performer smirked, handed the shoe box to his publicist, winked at my cousin, and then moved on to perform live. He didn't sign anything for anyone else in the crowd.

Now, I'm absolutely certain the singer could afford five thousand pairs of the same sneaker my cousin was wearing, but that is not the point. My cousin gave merit to this singer, even though the interaction lasted less than six seconds. My cousin got what he wanted, and made the singer feel important during his quest to get his attention. In turn, the singer gave my cousin what he wanted – an autograph and a moment in his life he will never forget.

As my cousin demonstrated, you can get anything you want.

Communicate the feeling that you are a progressive force to people, and that you improve everyone who intermingles with you. Radiate increase.

Let every part of your body communicate a relaxed poise that your "I Wants" are on their way to you. The Universe will take care of the rest. Always be cool, calm and collected. Words will not be required to speak this feeling to others. They will feel your energy of enhancement and will be attracted to you repeatedly.

Always remember to keep a level head and do not brag about your achievements. Keeping your ego in check is an exercise in modesty. It establishes a person's capacity to take charge of themselves.

The Universe wants to give you everything you desire. Your "I Wants" will grow quickly, and you will be astounded at the unanticipated benefits that will come to you. You will be able to up the ante and ask for bigger things. While doing this though, you must never forget the goals of your "I Want" list.

The Universe will never fail you. It will always present opportunity to the person who enhances others and who is moving in conformity with its law.

Summary

You cannot get something for nothing. You have to give in order to receive.

Taking something from someone and not giving

them greater worth of the thing is going against universal law. Always give more value for the thing you desire. You will certainly get more.

Give off the feeling that you are getting everything you desire in a cool, calm and collected manner. Never boast about your accomplishments.

Always know that the Universe and Subconscious Mind are working hand-in-hand to manifest your dreams.

Chapter 10

Setback, Schmetback

Life is a series of experiences, each one of which makes us bigger, even though sometimes it is hard to realize this. For the world was built to develop character, and we must learn that the setbacks and grieves which we endure help us in our marching onward.

— Henry Ford

Rule #76: No excuses. Play like a champion!

— Vince Vaughn

IN ORDER TO build up your determination and expand your mind, you will probably experience some knotty things in life. Negative people will say you cannot overcome a setback. It's unfortunate, but they will try to depress your dreams. You have the power to turn their gloom to your gain. If you command the Universe to benefit you and others, in spite of difficult conditions, you will always prevail. The person who is in tune with the Universe and their subconscious mind is the person who does the impossible.

Setbacks

If you come across a setback or deterrent during your journey, redefine it as an advantage. With self-belief and courage, the obstacles that look so frightening in the distance will get less significant as you move towards them. Do not waste any energy thinking that the obstacle will defeat you. You will absolutely find a way over, under, around or through the problem when it arises. The Universe will help you do this.

It takes the same effort to continue moving forward as it does to simply give up.

Learn from people who have stood in your shoes and figured out a way to do the impossible. The Universe gave these people everything they asked for because they had the will to succeed no matter what happened.

The people who get everything they want understand it takes the same effort to continue moving forward as it does to simply give up. How many dreams have never been realized because people did not have the perseverance to continue? How different would this world be if people actually enroll in the *Universe-ity* and use it for their benefit?

Because people lack gusto and determination in their decisions they often quit their goals after a few snubs. Just a couple of setbacks occur and it takes all the wind out of their sails. Then the dreaded "e" word comes in - *excuses*. These people come up with every excuse in the book to turn around and never advance.

Unmotivated people consistently try to justify to themselves why they can't get ahead. You will hear them moan - *It's too hard - I can't do it - I don't have the time - I'll do it tomorrow - I'm too tired - I'm too lazy - I don't feel like it - They won't let me - I don't have capital – I'm too sick* – and so on. These excuses are the poison that stops all progress in life. Why would *anyone* in this world make excuses to not get the thing they really desire? I cannot figure this out. They have every opportunity in the world to get anything they want, yet they whine about their current situation instead of doing something constructive about it. Ban *every* excuse from your mind once and for all. They will get you nowhere fast.

The person who accomplishes their dreams is the one who believes in the Universe, has command over their subconscious mind, lives life with sincere gratitude and gives more value to everyone around them. Successful people do not make excuses. If you want something badly enough, understand and believe you can get it no matter what is thrown in your path. The Universe likes to work with this mental attitude and will continuously make sure you triumph.

Do it Now

All that is being done in the Universe should be done *now*. Putting your goals off tomorrow or another day does not work. Aiming for a mere "want" and trying to avoid sacrificing sweat will not get you the thing you desire. What "wants" you will attain tomorrow is being established by the action you are taking today.

To quote the great Benjamin Franklin, "*He that is good for making excuses is seldom good for anything else.*" Don't give into irrational excuses like you have no opportunity or encouragement. Don't believe for an instant that no one is there to propel you to wealth or health. If there is something in your heart and you believe you are worth your substance, the Universe will light a path for you on your journey. It's so simple. All you have to do is just ask.

Summary

Setbacks are a part of life. Use their negative implications as a stepping stone around it to continue to reach your dreams.

Setbacks may look scary from a distance, but as you approach them you will find a way above, under, or through this setback.

No excuses! Ban all silly justifications from your life.

Tomorrow's reward will be worth today's hard work.

Outro

You are today the result of your thoughts of yesterday, and the many yesterdays proceeding it. You are forming today the mold for what you will be in the years to come.

— Robert Collier

You must present a P.M.A. (Positive Mental Attitude), for we all dance for freedom sake.

— Fishbone

WOULD LIKE TO sincerely thank you for completing this book and listening to what has worked for my friends, family, and me for so many years. You have taken the necessary steps to improve your life and your surroundings. I am grateful for having this chance to get to know you, and I hope you feel the same way about me.

Just Ask the Universe should be used to benefit you and the people you surround yourself with. Everything I wrote down on my original "I Want" list manifested into my life, and I added more. Some seeds are still growing. They are still in my garden. I think about them every day in an encouraging light. I know they are going to manifest in my life when the Universe is ready to deliver them. I still constantly add to my list, because my wants are constantly changing. I never delete things; I only add.

With a clear-cut list, a definitive connection with your subconscious mind, unwavering conviction, and meaningful gratitude, you will receive everything you ask for from the Universe. I sincerely hope you follow the rules in this book to manifest everything you wish.

You certainly deserve it.

Recommended Reading

As A Man Thinketh
Allen, James

Karma: The Ancient Science of Cause and Effect
Armstrong, Jeffrey

The Answer: Grow Any Business, Achieve Financial Freedom, and Live an Extraordinary Life
Assaraf, John

Thought Vibration – Law of Attraction in the Thought World
Atkinson, William Walker

The Art of Money Getting

Barnum, P.T.
The Magic of Believing
Bristol, Claude M.

The Universe Is Calling: Opening to the Divine through Prayer
Butterworth, Eric

The Power
Byrne, Rhonda

The Secret
Byrne, Rhonda

How to Stop Worrying and Start Living
Carnegie, Dale

The Genie Within: Your Subconscious Mind--How It Works and How to Use It
Carpenter, Harry W.

The Book of Secrets: Unlocking the Hidden Dimensions of Your Life
Chopra, Deepak

The Genie in Your Genes: Epigenetic Medicine and the New Biology of Intention
Church, Dawson

The Amazing Secrets of the Masters of the Far East
Collier, Robert

Be Rich!: The Science of Getting What You Want
Collier, Robert

The Life Magnet
Collier, Robert

Riches within Your Reach!
Collier, Robert

The Robert Collier Letter Book
Collier, Robert

The Secret of the Ages
Collier, Robert

Acres of Diamonds
Conwell, Russell

Choose Them Wisely: Thoughts Become Things!
Dooley, Mike

Infinite Possibilities: The Art of Living your Dreams
Dooley, Mike

Leveraging the Universe and Engaging the Magic
Dooley, Mike

Notes from the Universe: New Perspectives from an Old Friend
Dooley, Mike

Infinite Quest: Develop Your Psychic Intuition to Take Charge of Your Life
Edward, John

The Way to Wealth
Franklin, Benjamin

Prosperity
Fillmore, Charles

The Master Key System
Haanel, Charles F.

The Heart of the Buddha's Teaching
Hanh, Thich Nhat

Everyday Karma
Harra, Carmen

The Phenomenology of Spirit (The Phenomenology of Mind)
Hegel, Georg W. F.

Success Through A Positive Mental Attitude
Hill, Napoleon

Think and Grow Rich
Hill, Napoleon

Working with the Law
Holliwell, Raymond
Creative Mind and Success
Holmes, Ernest

The Hidden Power of the Bible
Holmes, Ernest

The Science of Mind
Holmes, Ernest

This Thing Called You
Holmes, Ernest

Write It Down, Make It Happen: Knowing What You Want and Getting It
Klauser, Henriette Anne

The Biology of Belief: Unleashing the Power of Consciousness, Matter, & Miracles
Lipton Ph.D., Bruce H.

Thoughts Are Things
Mulford, Prentice

Believe In Yourself
Murphy, Joseph

The Cosmic Energizer: Miracle Power of the Universe
Murphy, Joseph

How to Use the Laws of the Mind
Murphy, Joseph

The Miracle of Mind Dynamics: A New Way to Triumphant Living
Murphy, Joseph

The Power of Your Subconscious Mind
Murphy, Joseph

Psychic Perception: The Magic of Extrasensory Power (A miracles studies book)
Murphy, Joseph

Think Yourself Rich
Murphy, Joseph

Become a Better You: 7 Keys to Improving Your Life Every Day
Osteen, Joel

Good, Better, Blessed: Living with Purpose, Power and Passion
Osteen, Joel

It's Your Time: Activate Your Faith, Accomplish Your Dreams, and Increase in God's Favor
Osteen, Joel

Awaken the Giant Within: How to Take Immediate Control of Your Mental, Emotional, Physical, and Financial
Robbins, Anthony
Unlimited Power
Robbins, Anthony

The Game of Life and How to Play It
Shinn, Florence Scovel

Secret Door to Success
Shinn, Florence Scovel

Your Word Is Your Wand
Shinn, Florence Scovel

The Silva Mind Control Method
Silva, Jose

In Tune with the Infinite
Trine, Ralph

The Success System That Never Fails
Stone, W. Clement

The Science of Being Great
Wattles, Wallace D.

The Science of Being Well
Wattles, Wallace D.

The Science of Getting Rich
Wattles, Wallace D.

About the Author

WITH A DEGREE in English and a Masters in Business Administration, Michael Samuels has attracted everything into his life because he followed successful people and their thought processes. He has read and thoroughly tested hundreds of books on spirituality, self-improvement, and the metaphysical. The Universe has helped Michael run a highly successful family-owned business with offices all over the country. He currently lives in New York with his wife and son. *Just Ask the Universe* is his first book.

Michael would love to hear from you! Please email him your stories about how the Universe manifested "I wants" in your life.

Email: Michael@justasktheuniverse.com
Website: www.justasktheuniverse.com